The "S" Word

What Submission Is Not

Crystal Jones

The S Word: What Submission is NOT

All Rights Reserved.

Edited, formatted, and published by

Destiny House Publishing, LLC.

P.O. Box 19774

Detroit, MI 48219

inquiry@destinyhousepublishing.com

www.destinyhousepublishing.com

404.993.0830

Original printing Sept 2011

2nd Printing December 2021

Kingdom Graphic Design, LLC

Printed in the United States

ISBN: 9781936867035

Table of Contents

Foreword

In a world where women have been shoved to take a back seat to the attitudes of backward thinking men, we have witnessed a great resurging in how God uses women. Some have taken God's word and used it to keep women in a place that God never sanctioned. All the time, we are building our egos. I say egos because we couldn't possibly build —a church without women.

Certainly, I don't discount the role of submission in the church. It is the key to what God will do, for and through us, both men and women. For we all must embrace submission.

In *The S Word*, you will see the intent of God's heart concerning submission. It's not what you think. This book will give you a balanced look at submission, as God intended for us. Within these pages you will find principles that liberate the soul and turn hearts back toward God.

Men don't have to be intimidated by this book. When your wife finds purpose through submission, it will create the kind of wife that you will cherish. So I challenge you to read this book and cheer on the women in your lives.

Crystal is a woman who lives within the pages of this book. I should know, I am her husband and best friend. She is a humble and submitted wife to me and a submitted daughter to the Lord.

So, to the ladies, enjoy this book as God speaks to your heart. Allow Him to take you on a journey to true freedom.

-Apostle Oscar Jones, Overseer & Founder: Greater Works Family Ministries, The Love Culture Christian Center, Agape International Association of Churches & Parachurches, and Marriage For A Lifetime Ministries

Acknowledgments

I give thanks to my most Faithful Lord for your
inspiration andguidance in writing this book
and leading my life.

Loads of gratitude to my amazing husband of 40
years, Apostle Oscar Jones for all your love and
support. You are the best husband on theplanet. It is
indeed an honor to be your wife.

Dedications

I lovingly dedicate this book to all the lovely ladies of WOW! (Women of Wisdom) and LOL (Ladies of Love):

You ladies inspire me. I celebrate you for being the beautiful, wonderful daughters that you are. May the Lord continue to showyou all that is in you, so that you can share it with the world. I love you all.

CHAPTER 1

A Submitted Savior

But made himself of no reputation, and took upon him the form of a servant, and was made in the likeness of men: and being found in fashion as a man, he humbled himself, and became obedient unto death, even the death of the cross.

Philippians 2:7-8

⌘

The word submission often makes the average Christian woman cringe. Because the word has been misused and abused in the church over the years to get women to do whatever a husband demanded.

There were no requirements of that same husband. Men barked orders at their wives and declared, I am the head! As if that meant, "You must do everything I say". And if a wife disagreed, it was as if all of heaven would open up and gasp at her defiance. She was surely a candidate for hell. God is so much smarter than what we as humans make him out to be.

Not only did Jesus clearly spell out what true submission is in His word, but He demonstrated submission to us. He took on humanity's garment and walked the earth completely yielding to the Father. In fact, scripture says, that this mind that Jesus had, should be in all of us (Phil 2:5-8). He was in the form of God, but left His heavenly position for one of a human servant. He was seen as a mere man. Of course, He was much more than that. Yet, He gave it all up; because he regarded sinners (his bride) as more important than Himself. He was just as concerned with our needs as with his own.

He did not throw fits demanding to be obeyed. He didn't

continue to stress to us (his bride) that He is the Head. He is fully aware of who He is. He doesn't feel a need to defend himself or protect his ego. And this love cost Him his life. Yet He loved enough to die for His bride. And with this loving kindness He drew us into submission.

The church yielded freely out of awe for such a profound love.She was humbled by a love so great and so peculiar that her submission was the least she could render.

However, this is not what we were presented, when we were taught submission. We have been taught that submission is one sided and gender specific: for women only. We have beentaught that submission could be demanded. We've also been instructed that submission meant a lot of things that it didn't.The list goes on and on.

So how did we get so far from the truth?

Let's take a look at Ephesians 5:22-24 in an attempt to see how we've gone askew. This scripture was the golden rule, the catalyst for all of this ado; because it was taken out of context and misinterpreted.

Wives submit yourselves unto your own husbands, as unto the Lord. For the husband is the head of the wife, even as Christ is the head of the church: and he is the savior of the body. Therefore as the church is subject unto Christ, so let the wives be to their own husbands in every thing. Ephesians 5:22-24

We can only clearly understand scripture in its proper context. The church handicaps itself when we do not properly apply scripture. God wants us to be healthy and whole. This requires proper application of the Word. Let's not stop at verse 24. Let us seek the heart of God from which this whole idea of submission sprung.

Remember that old woman Jezebel? She was a vile character. In I Kings 21, Naboth refused to sell his property to Ahab because of inheritance regulations of the law of Moses.

King Ahab went whining to his evil wife. She wrote letters in her husband's name, gathered men to lie on Naboth, saying that he had blasphemed God and the king. She then had him stoned and took his land. Jezebel was a woman heavily into pagan idolatry. She was a worshiper of the Phoenician god, Baal. She corrupted the king and the nation. Because of her wicked legacy, every strong or confident woman is, at times, inappropriately labeled a Jezebel. Some, so easily, sling accusations at women, attaching this unwanted tag to us.

Why is it that we can't seem to shake her? I think that it has to do with our prejudices. Whenever we have a bias against a people or culture, we usually link them to the worst of their breed. Think about it. Christians get branded by the kooks that burn down abortion clinics. Muslims are identified with jihad terrorists. African-Americans are lumped together with gang-bangers. And the list continues.

So when it comes to strong, godly women, we all get incorrectly classified as a Jezebel. Men… and even some women get intimidated and grab hold to these biases. And we can't seem to move further.

But what if we did go further…? Just what if we did eat the whole roll? The very next scripture in verse 25 says, *Husbands love your wives even as Christ also loved the church and gave himself for it;* There *is* a requirement of husbands. Husbands ought to love their wives like Christ loves the church. What a novel concept: a husband is to love his wife like Jesus loves the church. Interesting.

The Greek word for love is agape which denotes a sacrificial love without receiving anything in return. Whether she yields or not, hubby is to love his bride.

There is no sacrifice that a husband should not be willing to make for his bride.

Consider the Christ who knew no sin but became sin for us. He took sin's penalty despite His innocence. Even in the midst of Him laying down His life, His bride continued to revile him and mock him. And He stayed on that cross lovingly taking her place and petitioning the Father not to layit to her charge. My, how the divorce rate would drop if men really loved their wives like that; giving up everything for her - even his life.

And yet there is more, look at verse 26-29: That he might sanctify and cleanse it with the washing of water by the word. That he might present it to himself a glorious church, not having spot of wrinkle, or any such thing: but that it should be holy and without blemish. So ought men to love their wives as their own bodies. He that loveth his wife loveth himself. For no man ever yet hated his own flesh; but nourisheth and cherisheth it, even as the Lord the church.

Yes, His bride is in need of cleansing. But Christ takes personal responsibility for his bride. His love will cover her. He will wash her. And He will present her back to himself.

Shouldn't husbands take spiritual responsibility for their wives, if he is truly her head? Husbands have received these women who have been wounded, abused, and dirtied by the world.

She may have been scarred by her parents, former lovers, siblings, and society as a whole. As a man receives God's love, he is in position to offer that back to His wife, who may be shattered and torn. He can love her to wholeness, emulating Christ.

As much attention as the husband gives to himself, he must give to his wife. He can show that he loves himself by loving her first. Sacrificial love benefits both the giver and the receiver. The wife profits from the love of her husband in that she is granted forgiveness and mercy. She is treated tenderly. She is loved without condition. But the husband also benefits from his love in obtaining a purified bride as she is transformed by His love.

Verses 30-33 read: For we are members of his body, of his flesh and of his bones. For this cause shall a man leave his father and mother and shall be joined unto his wife and they two shall be one flesh. This is a great mystery: but I speak concerning Christ and thechurch. Nevertheless let every one of you in particular so love his wife even as himself; and the wife see that she reverence her husband.

This is a great mystery. For centuries, men have misunderstood what marriage was all about... And we lost the essence of what God wanted us to understand. We approached marriage with such a secular view that we could not even begin to grasp what God wanted to reveal to us. Consequently, marriages fail, are cold and embittered, because everyone is seeking his own way.

God is love. And He expects the two to become one. This in itself is submission. The whole mystery of marriage is that marriage is ministry. It's about two individuals stepping outside of themselves and serving the other. Spouses should seek the highest good; in always seeking the best interest of the relationship - not the individual. Marriage is the ultimate example of selflessness. It's a mystery, because we are either in darkness and the god of this world has blinded our eyes or we have simply closed our eyes to truth.

It is time for revelation.

Submission is not a feminine word. If we really take a good look at scripture, there is a call to every believer male and female to *submit* to the will of God. James 4:6-7 reads, but hegiveth more grace. Wherefore he saith, God resisteth the proud, but giveth grace unto the humble. **Submit yourselves therefore to God**. Resist the devil, and he will flee from you.

God is speaking to all people here. Submission is a holy word.It is to be embraced by all who belong to God; male and female. Just as it is required of women *and* men, it is requiredof wives *and* husbands. If we look at the pretext of our original Ephesians passage, the scripture reads in

Ephesians 5:21

> Submitting yourselves one to another in the fear of
> God.

Ah… Husbands, too, need to submit to their wives. If we take a walk through Genesis, we can see in the beginning, God calls the wife, the helper. That word means a rescuer beside him. How can she help if her husband never positions himself to submit to his wife? He will never receive what she has to say or to offer. He must be willing to submit to help.

It is my intent to change the mindset of so many who misunderstand what God intends. The ideal relationship is one based on love, trust and mutual respect where both partners complement each other.

At the same time, clearly understand, I am not advocating that wives rebel against their husband's authority. I do believe that the husband is the head of the wife. And that the wife should respect and honor her one flesh partner.

However, the instruction on submission has not always been presented in an impartial manner. I want to offer a more balanced perspective than what I've seen and heard in the past.

In the subsequent chapters, I hope to reveal what true submission is and what submission is not. At the end of each chapter, you will find questions to ponder and a notes section to record those thoughts. Follow me as we take this journey.

Notes:

CHAPTER 2

Submission is never sinful.

Colossians 3:18 Wives, submit yourselves unto your own husbands, as it is fit in the Lord.

⌘

Women have been instructed to obey their husbands at all costs. This is certainly *not* the will of God. Submission is always subject to the Lord. Wives are to submit to husbands….<u>as unto the Lord </u>(Eph 5:22). God is always due first obedience. A husband takes second position to Christ…always and under every circumstance. So if there is a contradiction, God always wins. When Peter and the disciples were threatened about teaching in the name of Jesus, they boldly proclaimed. "We ought to obey God rather than men" (Acts 5:29). And that is as it should be.

My husband and I have counseled many women who have been asked to sin against God by their Christian husbands. This may be hard to believe. But it is more prevalent than we realize. Women are torn between duty to God and duty to their husbands. This ungodly tug of war is manipulation wielded by a man who is insecure and lacks understanding. God is holy and righteous and He begets a holy and righteous people. It is quite offensive to the Lord to manipulate His Holy scriptures for wicked purposes. The person who does this will not go unpunished. Husbands have been guilty.

Wives are sometimes unsure where the line is drawn. But let's make it clear. At **no time,** should a wife agree with her husband to sin against God. Let us take a look at one who did.

But a certain man named Ananias, with Sapphira his wife, sold a possession, And kept back part of the price, his wife also being privy to it, and brought a certain part and laid it at the apostles' feet.

But Peter said, Ananias, why hath Satan filled thine heart to lie to the Holy Ghost, and to keep back part of the price of the land? While it remained, was it not thine own? And after it was sold was it not in thine own power? why hast thou conceived this thing in thine heart? Thou hast not lied unto men, but unto God. And Ananias hearing these words fell down, and gave up the ghost: and great fear came on all them that heard these things. And the young men arose, wound him up and carried him out, and buried him.

And it was about the space of three hours after, when his wife, not knowing what was done came in. And Peter answered unto her, "Tell me whether ye sold the land for so much?" And she said, "Yea for so much". Then Peter said unto her, *How is it that ye have agreed together to tempt the Spirit of the Lord?"* Behold the feet of them which have buried thy husband are at the door, and shall carry thee out.

Then fell she down straightway at his feet and yielded up the ghost: and the young men came in, and found her dead, and, carrying her forth, buried her by her husband. (Acts 5:1-10).

The wife in this passage, Sapphira, got the same punishment as her head because she agreed with him to sin against God. A woman's allegiance to her spouse must end at sin. Questions arise concerning tithing, going to church, or participating in other suspect activity, etc. Those doubts are answered by simply following the Word of God. For example, if a husband decides to connect cable or utilities illegally, his wife should not agree or participate in this type of activity. This is an act of theft. The Bible clearly says, "Thou shalt not steal." (Exodus 20:15).

Another example would be if a husband cheats on the couple's income taxes and/or claims a child they are not entitled to claim. The wife should withhold her signature.

One of the most common questions we have received is "Should I tithe if my husband doesn't agree?" Again, we have to go to the scriptures. Refusing to tithe is robbing or stealing from God. "Will a man rob God? Yet ye have robbed me. But ye say wherein have we robbed thee? In tithes and offerings." (Malachi 3:8). Therefore if a wife has her own income, she should follow God's word. Her submission must be to God, first.

In more serious cases, a wife should not allow her husband to abuse or molest a child. She cannot hide behind a plea of submission. Her inaction is consent. She must not concede to these ungodly acts. If she does, she, too, is guilty.

Husbands do not have a right to demand that their wives violate God's principles. The compromising wife will be judged by God, along with her husband. Every man and woman will be held accountable for his/her own sins. We must always follow God's Word above all others. A wife that cooperates in her husband's sin will be judged as if the sin originated with her: just as Sapphira was. There is no free pass for obeying a husband. We are to obey man when man agrees with God.

When the Scripture speaks of wives obeying and submitting to their husbands, it does not mean that every wife must obey her husband at every single demand. She, as well as he, is responsible to obey what the Spirit gives each to do.

A wife should never violate God's word to please her husband. God doesn't require it. In fact, His word forbids it. A woman must hold onto her integrity no matter what her husband requests.

Self-examination

1. Why should you refuse to submit to sin?

2. Who do you think is at the root of coaxing you to sin?

3. What do you think would have happened had Sapphira told Ananias that she was not going to cooperate with him?

4. Do you have the courage to stand for holiness? Why or Why not?

Notes:

_____

_____

_____

_____

_____

_____

_____

_____

_____

_____

_____

_____

_____

_____

_____

_____

CHAPTER 3

Submission does not mean Shielding

He that covereth his sins shall not prosper: but whoso confesseth and forsaketh them shall have mercy. Proverbs 28:13

⌘

The scripture says; Therefore as the church is subject unto Christ, so let the wives be to their own husbands in **every thing** (Eph 5:24). Any spiritual leader worth his weight in salt will tell you that this is not a literal translation. The scripture says **as** the church is subject to Christ. That is an important lead in. Women are to submit as long as her submission does not go against the word or character of God.

A wife has no responsibility to cover up her husband's improprieties. Too many times, men of God get caught up in addictions or destructive behaviors. To make matters worse, they demand that their wives not share it with anyone. It is counter-productive to participate in or comply with such a request. God does not expect it.

I Timothy 5:22 reads, Lay hands suddenly on no man, *neither be partaker of other men's sins: keep thyself pure.* The wife becomes a participator in her husband sins when she covers up for him. In our culture, if a person aids and abets a person in a crime, he is just as guilty as the perpetrator; he is called an accessory or accomplice to the crime.

A spouse should be careful not to purchase alcohol, drugs, etc. for her husband. It is important that she doesn't become his enabler. An enabler is someone who provides the resources, authority, or opportunity to continue in harmful behavior to a person with addictive behavior. This is an unhealthy position and it is detrimental to the marriage.

The struggle often ensues because the wife wants to remain loyal to her husband. However, she must understand that loyalty always does what is in the best interest of the other party. It is not in a husband's best interest for a wife to promote or cover his sin.

He that covereth his sins shall not prosper: but whoso confesseth and forsaketh them shall have mercy (Proverbs 28:13).

Love exposes him; so that he can get the help he needs. If a wife continues to hide or help her husband hide his sin, he will continue in it. There is no motivation for him to quit. He can only get help if that sin is uncovered. Gambling, pornography, drug abuse, uncontrolled anger, alcoholism, sexual sins, etc. are all destructive behaviors.

Sometimes, men will insist that their wives 'just pray' for them. Women should seek help for their husbands through prayer *and* human intervention. Of course, prayer is needed and powerfully effective. However, the husband will also need to be held accountable. Accountability is so important in the process of breaking addictions. The Bible says we ought to confess our faults one to another so that we can be healed. So while prayer is great and powerfully effective. A wife also needs to bring in someone to hold her husband accountable. If a wife shields her husband's secrets, she is unwittingly aiding him in his self-destruction.

When looking to bring to light those things done in darkness, the lines can be blurry in what to disclose and what not to disclose. After seeking God, a wife should consult her pastor/spiritual leader for guidance. The person that one chooses to confide in should be selected with care. It should be a person mature enough to handle such sensitive information.

Certainly, a wife should NOT expose her husband to any and every one. Her whole objective is to be what God intended, —the helper. She wants her husband to get the help he so desperately needs.

Sometimes a wife covers for her husband because she is ashamed. Shame is only beneficial to provoke us out of sin into righteousness. We should be ashamed of our own actions when they offend God. Even with that, after repentance, we should not remain in a place of shame.

However, to be ashamed because of someone else's actions is unhealthy and not beneficial. Shame can be used as a powerful tool of the enemy to keep us from progress and purpose. Shame can cause you to be immobile. Don't allow your union to be shamed into disintegration. Seek the help you need to save your marriage.

On the other hand, wives need to understand that there is a difference between exposing sins and exposing faults. If a husband is a poor money manager, that is a fault; not a sin. Faults should certainly be covered by the wife. However, if he is stealing money from his employer, that is a sin. Do not cover his sin. To clearly determine if something is a fault or a sin, ask the question, —What does the Word say about this behavior? Will this thing bring irreparable harm to our family? Most importantly, a wife should seek godly counsel. The Bible encourages us, in the multitude of counsel, there is safety.

Self-examination

1. Define the word loyalty:

2. Cite an example of a loyal relationship in scripture. What makes it special?

3. Have you ever covered for someone and later regretted it?

4. Recall a relationship where you wish that someone (friend or family member) had been exposed to get help.

5. Give an ungodly example of loyalty in scripture.

Notes:

Chapter 4

Submission does not mean you are the Sacrificial Lamb

And I saw a strong angel proclaiming with a loud voice, Who is worthy to open the book, and to loose the seals thereof? And no man in heaven, nor in earth, neither under the earth, was able to open the book, neither to look thereon. And I wept much, because no man was found worthy to open and to read the book, neither to look thereon. And one of the elders saith unto me, Weep not: behold, the Lion of the tribe of Judah, the Root of David, hath prevailed to open the book, and to loose the seven seals thereof. Revelation 5:2-6

⌘

God never intended for women to be abused. Abuse is an ugly sin. Wounded men often take out their insecurities and frustrations on their wives and vulnerable children. They insist that their victims deserved it because of some behavior on their part. He uses fear, shame, intimidation and guilt to gain control. A batterer rarely takes responsibility for his own actions. He sees himself as chastising his wife for her ill behavior. The problem is the chastiser is the guilty one. He is the one ill.

God never intended that men should control or dominate their wives. Christ never controls or dominates humankind. And He sets the example of how men ought to love their wives.

Even if the wife has done wrong, it is not the place of the husband to chastise her. He cannot take the place of God. Man is too evil to be entrusted with such power. Because God is love, He has the right to chasten us. We belong to Him. Our sin was vile and heinous in the sight of God. It deserved to be punished. Because God is so holy, sin demanded punishment. So God put His loving plan into action.

His plan was to take the punishment on himself. Jesus is the Lamb of God that was slain for us. He sacrificed Himself so that we would not have to receive the retribution. He was beaten, bruised, afflicted, and wounded all for the sake of man's sin. He was the only One qualified because He was sinless.

God does not ask any wife to become a martyr to her spouse. He does not ask you to become a sacrificial lamb. No one else is qualified, because the lamb must be spotless. Therefore a wife cannot take that position in her husband's life.

Scripture does not support a wife taking licks for the sake of submission. The husband's role is to protect and nurture his wife, not demean and abuse her. This is not at all pleasing to God. Christ never abuses the church. And He does not expect spouses to stay in these types of dangerous situations. A wife should not remain in any harmful situation. She absolutely must remove herself and any children.

Let me state what is obvious to most of us - it is **never** acceptable or excusable for a man to slap, kick, bite, beat, push, punch, stump or inflict ANY type of physical harm upon his wife. It is not God's will for any of his children to be abused. God has called us to peace. His sacrifice rescued us from the abuser and accuser.

Unfortunately, battered women tend to stay in abusive relationships for many reasons. She may feel like she has no other recourse, but this is a trick of the enemy. There is no good reason for her to put her life at risk.

Inaction promotes his dysfunctional behavior. A battered wife should remove herself from the danger. She should seek safety for herself and her children.

Many of these women talk themselves into staying by thinking that she can talk to him...one more time. However, the scriptures warn, Do not try to reason with an angry man (Prov 22:24).

She may think, If I just stay and pray for him, maybe he will change. She absolutely should pray for her husband until he gets the help he needs. However she must pray from a distance. God is still able to hear her.

It is important for her to recognize that she is not the one who can help her husband. She is the target of his abuse. His help must come from outside the marriage. So she must love him enough to help him stop the abuse, by removing herself from the home. Her husband is a man in pain. And inflicting his pain on his spouse demonstrates his need for intervention.

This is also true about the husband who verbally abuses his wife. A wife is not commanded to stand there and take him cursing at her. She should remove herself from such abuse. The Bible says that words are spirit. So she must guard herself from such ungodly attacks.

It is against the Word of God for a husband to call his wife names and hurl insults at her. A wife does not have to receive those poisonous words as an act of submission. This is NOT holy submission. How can she agree with what God says about her *and* what her husband says? If they conflict, she must believe the Word. She should not allow herself to be verbally abused. She can leave the room, the house, or environment until a later time when they can talk reasonably. If a husband is consistently verbally abusive, his wife should insist that they go for counseling. If he refuses, she needs to remove herself from the abuse until he is ready to acquiesce. He must allow himself to be held accountable.

The abused wife must demonstrate a healthy love for herself and her husband. Her love becomes toxic when she refuses to leave. An abusive husband needs to take a good long hard look at himself. And this is often difficult when the wife stays in the abusive environment.

She needs to get back into a healthy emotional and spiritual place. She will need her own individualized Christian counseling to be able to see herself as God sees her. Her self-image needs to be built up through the Word.

When traveling on an airplane, the flight attendant gives instructions in case of an emergency. She says that in the event there is a drop in cabin pressure, the oxygen mask will drop down. She further encourages passengers to always secure their own masks before helping anyone else, including children. It might seem selfish. But think about it, if you can't breathe, how can you help anyone else?

I think this is also relevant in the case of abuse. A wife cannot help her family until she gets help for herself. If she secures her own oxygen mask first, this is the most selfless and loving act she can render to her family.

She needs to hear God's loving and affirming voice. She needs to understand that God loves and accepts her just as she is. And that she has a lot to offer the body of Christ. She also must communicate clearly to her children that abuse is not who God is or what He accepts. It is important that we don't paint a false picture of God's character.

As women of God, our submission is always *as unto the Lord.* If a husband requires something against the very nature of God, wives are not obligated to concede.

His requests should never demean his one flesh partner. Scripture is clear; a husband's prayers are hindered if he does not treat his wife properly (I Peter 3:7).

If you know someone or suspect that someone is a victim of domestic violence, pray for her/him. Be supportive. Reach out to them. Offer a way to escape this life of torment.

If you are a victim of domestic violence, act immediately. Call the National Domestic Violence Hotline at 1-800-799-SAFE

(7233). They will direct you to safe places in your area where you can seek help.

Self-examination

1. Do you know or suspect that someone you know is being abused? Can you help?

2. Read St. John 8:1-11. What do you think Jesus is thinking while he is writing?

3. How does St. John 8:1-11 tell us that we are to respond to other's sins?

4. Do you think that verbal abuse is less harmful than physical abuse? Why?

5. Is it ever okay for a husband to curse out his wife? If so, under what circumstances?

Notes:

Chapter 5

Submission does not mean Second-rate

So God created mankind in his own image, in the image of God he created them; male and female he created them. Genesis 1:27 NIV

⌘

Women have been treated as second class citizens in nearly every culture. African women are circumcised to prevent them from experiencing sexual pleasure. In India, women are thought to be a curse if her husband dies. In other cultures, a woman cannot be in public unless there is a man with her. Some require that the wife walk behind her husband. There is even the thought that every female is beneath every male in religious circles. How does the world come up with such extreme ideas?

It all started in the garden when God was meting out curses. "And I will put **enmity between thee and the woman**, and between thy seed and her seed; it shall bruise thy head, and thou shalt bruise his heel." Genesis 3:15

Of course, this spoke to Jesus as the Conqueror. But how would Jesus enter the earth? Through the "woman". Satan was not a happy camper. Just as he sent out a decree to kill all babies under the age of 2 to try to rid the earth of the Messiah (So dumb). I believed he has been behind the all-out attack against the female. His b e s t and most effective weapon has been to poison mankind against her. Keep her quiet. Keep her in her place. Keep her under. As a result, women have been oppressed in almost every avenue: politics, business, education, church, etc.

Certainly, **both** men and women have a call to submit to spiritual and natural authority; as long as that authority does not conflict with the God we serve. God made it clear that both mothers and fathers (which are female and male) are to be treated with equal respect (Exodus 20:12).

God created male *and female* in His own image. We do not serve a God who sees women as second-class citizens. In the beginning, God created the wife to rule alongside her husband. She is an important part of a dynamic team.

They were both extended dominion and authority. Genesis 1:27-28 So God created mankind in his own image, in the image of God he created them; male *and female* he created them. God blessed *them* and said to *them*, "Be fruitful and increase in number; fill the earth and subdue it. Rule over the fish in the sea and the birds in the sky and over every living creature that moves on the ground."

Femininity is not a curse. It is a wonderful blessing. A woman has full rights and benefits in the kingdom of God. Woman was never an after-thought. She was always a part of God's heart and master plan. He expected her to rule beside Adam. And today she still has a significant role in the Kingdom. God says, there is neither male nor female in the realm of the Spirit. He pours out His spirit on His sons *and his daughters*.

God did not create woman as second class. She is in the class of humanity. Her gender does not make her less important to God. She is completely equal in her access to salvation through Jesus Christ.

The problem that some people make is thinking that being equal means dismissing the call to submit. This is a wrong idea. Submission is not in opposition to equality. Jesus proved you can hold both positions at the same time. Jesus is both equal to God and submitted to Him.

Let this mind be in you, which was also in Christ Jesus: Who being in the form of God, thought it not robbery to be equal with God: But made himself of no reputation, and took upon him the form of a servant, and was made in the likeness of men: And being found in fashion as a man, he humbled **himself**, and became obedient unto death, even the death of the cross. Philippians 2:5-8 KJV

Christ's submission to the Father does not make him inferior. The Father, Son, and Holy Spirit are all 100% God. They are not a fraction of God. The differences in the Godhead are only in function. Jesus is fully God (Colossians 2:9). In the same way, a woman's submission to her husband does not make her inferior to him. She is fully human. Her role or function is different.

Certainly women cannot do everything that men can do; just

as men can't do everything that women can do. Women and men are vastly different. This is a good thing. God intended that we would celebrate our differences and complement one another. God put a portion of his image in both sexes. So neither is lesser than the other. We need both. If it is not good for man to be without the woman, it means she is necessary. She is relevant. She is not secondary.

Self-examination

1. Why is it not good for the man to be alone?

2. Did you assume that God values men more than women? How has that affected your faith?

3. Have you ever been treated inferior by a man because you are female? Explain.

4. Has it affected your life?

5. How did Jesus interact with women?

Notes:

CHAPTER 6

Submission is not Slavery

For, brethren, ye have been called unto liberty; only use not liberty for an occasion to the flesh, but by love serve one another. Galatians 5:13

⌘

Submission is a dirty word to many women because of the way it has been misused. In its presentation, there was very little difference to human slavery. It meant a loss of a woman's rights and privileges. Because she is married, she must allow her husband to do whatever he wants, whenever he wants. She must sit passively and quietly by and take whatever he decides to dish out. Can you imagine being subject to every whim of a man? That does sound pretty scary. There is no wonder women have resisted this interpretation of submission for so many years. Even King David said, I am in a great strait: let me fall now into the hand of the Lord; for very great are his mercies: *but let me not fall into the hand of men.* I Chronicles 21:13

Submission to a husband does not mean a woman is to be a slave and in bondage to that man. Submission means to yield or "to set yourself under." It's a voluntary act of love. Just as we intentionally surrender our wills to God because of the love relationship we have with Him. This is what was meant by wives submitting themselves to their husbands.

Women are not slaves. He who the Son sets free is free indeed. Men and women are called to liberty. God has made us all free and gifted us with a free will. So women have the capacity to make choices. She has the ability to agree or disagree. She has the power to reason and think for herself.

As in previous chapters, understand that women are not subject to any and every direction of her husband.

A husband cannot force his wife to work outside the home. The scriptures call for the husband to provide for the family. As the leader, it is his job to take care of his family. However a submissive wife may *want* to help her husband because of her love for him and her family. She *chooses* to do this. And she is motivated by love, not by orders. In Proverbs 31, we see the virtuous wife was very industrious. She bought and sold land, she worked diligently with her hands, engaged in trading, etc. She was not coerced. The acrostic poem leads us to see her as one who was provoked by her love for God and her love for her family.

God does not give men a right to demand any and every action from his wife. A husband's charge is to love his wife like Christ loves his bride, the church. He leaves her free will completely intact. He consistently tells her to choose. She is drawn to choose Him because of his loving-kindness. Kind husbands get far more than harsh ones.

A wife is not man's personal property. He cannot treat her harshly by demanding services from her. She belongs to God.

One husband attempted to humiliate his wife publicly by

yelling at her to stop talking and go inside the home and cook his dinner. This was done in front of family and friends. This is rude and disrespectful behavior; and not the spirit that God intends or expects.

Another area, that is especially problematic, is in the bedroom. Men, often demand that their wives fulfill their sexual longings regardless of her feelings. **God never endorses selfishness.** I Corinthians 7:3-5, it reads, Let the husband render unto the wife due benevolence: and likewise also the wife unto the husband. The wife hath not power of her own body, but the husband: and likewise also the husband hath not power of his own body, but the wife. Defraud ye not one the other, except it be with consent for atime, that ye may give yourselves to fasting and prayer; and come together again, that Satan tempt you not for your incontinency.

Paul is speaking to husbands and wives about mutually satisfying one another. Each verse speaks to both partners. Paul is giving principles for married life in regards to keeping the marriage bed clean. He does not in any way make the wife, a sex slave in this passage.

His main statement is this, it is a good practice for married couples to come together as often as the two desire, to keep themselves from sexual sin. He says, but this is not a commandment. So he is saying practice this, but don't use it as a law. Paul understood there would be times when a woman would not be able to come together with her husband.

For example:

- When she is menstruating

- After giving birth

- After surgery

- When she is experiencing female complications

- When she is ill

- When she is exhausted

- When she is emotionally bleeding

A wise husband is sensitive and sympathetic to his wife. I Peter 3:7 admonishes husbands to dwell with their wives according to knowledge, giving honor unto the wife, as unto the weaker vessel, and as being heirs together of the grace of life; that your prayers be not hindered.

Of course, this is not a free pass for a wife to be manipulative to withhold sex from her husband. God is always interested in our motives. However, husbands should respect and honor their wives and not treat them as if they are personal property. A husband does not have a right to rape his wife. If a wife cannot participate sexually for a season, then her husband needs to be sensitive and patient enough to allow her time for healing and restoration. If that period of time is longer than he anticipated or she refuses for any other reason, he still has no right to take sex from her. His first reaction should be one of prayer. He should talk to his wife to understand why she iswhere she is. If that does not work, he should seek counseling.

Self-examination

1. Have you ever withheld sex from your husband? Was God in agreement?

2. What did Paul mean when he said the husband's body belongs to the wife and the wife's body belongs to the husband?

3. In I Chronicles 21:13, what did King David mean?

4. Do you view submission as slavery? Why?

5. Explain the following verses:

   St John 8:36

   Galatians 5:1

   Luke 4:18

Notes:

CHAPTER 7

Submission does not mean Silence

But speaking the truth in love, may grow up into him in all things, which is the head, even Christ. Ephesians 4:15

⌘

Submission does not mean that you do not have a voice. On the contrary, you do have a voice with God and with your husband. Too often, we hear well-meaning **teachers** misinterpret the scripture that says women ought to keep silent in the church. The lesson is presented in a way to cause us to think that women cannot speak, teach, pray, give a word, etc. She should do nothing in the church, other than listen and give her tithes and offerings.

On the contrary, Paul did not intend for us to come up with that interpretation. He had many female co-laborers in his company. His culture and time dictated that he write such a letter to the Corinthian church. The custom did not allow for genders to sit together. The men sat on one side and women on the other. The church was a little out of hand. Women were asking their husbands questions across the room.

So we read in I Cor 14:33-35: For God is not a God of disorder but of peace. As in all the congregations of the saints, women should remain silent in the churches. They are not allowed to speak, but must be in submission, as the Law says. If they want to inquire about something, they should ask their own husbands at home; for it is disgraceful for a woman to speak in the church.

The women were interrupting the order of worship. So Paul

was speaking to the disorder. He was <u>not</u> giving a command that no woman should ever speak in the church or to men.

How do we know this? Because Paul commended many women that worked with him in the Gospel (Romans 16:1-15). He also told the elder women to teach the younger. (Titus 2:4)

It does not make sense that a woman can speak to a majestic omnipotent God but is forbidden to speak to men concerning her God.

Let 's take a deeper look at scripture; Pilate's wife gives him advice regarding Jesus.

When he was set down on the judgment seat, his wife sent unto him,saying have thou nothing to do with that just man: for I have suffered many things this day in a dream because of him. (St. Matthew 27:19).

God gave the wife of Pilate a dream about Jesus and she shared it with her husband. He listened and washed his hands of the act of Jesus' crucifixion.

Over the issue of Hagar, Abraham is commanded by God to listen to Sarah and to accept her understanding regarding the situation.

"...Cast out this bondwoman and her son: for the son of this bondwoman shall not be heir with my son, even with Isaac. And the thing was very grievous in Abraham's sight because of his son. And God said unto Abraham, let it not be grievous in thy sight because of the lad, and because of thy bondwoman; *in all that Sarah hath said unto thee, hearken unto her voice;* for in Isaac shall thy seed be called." Genesis 21:10-12

This is especially noteworthy because Sarah was the one who gave Abraham incorrect instruction concerning sleeping with Hagar, in the first place. Yet, God tells Abraham to listen to her and obey her instruction. He doesn't forbid her from speaking again, because she made a mistake.

God looks at a husband and wife as a team of one. The two are one flesh. So he will give the wife a word just as quickly as the husband. God spoke to Mary about Jesus before he spoke to Joseph.

As helper to her mate, a wife should feel free to speak what is on her heart, even if it is not accepted. God gives her the ability to speak. She should use that for His glory.

However she must be careful that she does not take on the spirit that we are warning against. She should NOT become controlling and dogmatic about the word that God has given her. She should stand back and let her husband do with the word what he wills.

Once a wife delivers what God has spoken, she must allow

her husband to be free to obey or not. She shouldn't get angry if he doesn't follow through on the word. Neither should she challenge him on it. She's done her part as helper by releasing the word to her husband. Her job is done. She does not have an assignment to make him obey; no matter how often it is disregarded.

It is also important that she does not shut down. She must continue to obey God. Often disobedience breeds more disobedience. So she must be careful. If her spouse is disobedient, she may fall into disobedience with him by refusing to deliver another word. Or by demonstrating ungodly behavior because she is angry. It is an expression of pride.

As a woman of God, she must continue speaking in love and wisdom. She needs to be careful about nagging, or of being argumentative. It is better to dwell in a corner of the housetop than with a brawling woman in a wide house. (Proverbs 21:9, 19)

It is easy to fall prey to self-righteousness. Avoid saying, I told you so. She must speak softly. Her words should be seasoned with grace. Her primary purpose is **not** to prove her husband wrong, but to be his helper and support.

Every wise woman buildeth her house: but the foolish plucketh it down with her hands. Proverbs 14:1

God gives the wife a voice to speak in the church and at home. She is to use it with wisdom. He expects that she will speak up with confidence at His nudging.

If a husband does not respond to his wife, when she releases a word from the Lord, he is not exercising wisdom. He will have to eat the fruit of his pride. His wife will always have a voice with God if she remains faithful. She can always go over her husband's head by going down on her knees in prayer.

Self-examination

1. Read Romans 16: 1-15. List the women that Paul mentions.

2. For what qualities does Paul commend these women?

3. Why did Paul say, let the women keep silent?

4. Have you ever kept silent when God told you to speak? Why?

5. When the scriptures say that women are to keep silent in the church, was does that mean to you?

Notes:

Chapter 8

Submission does not mean you are Stripped.

But you are a chosen people, a royal priesthood, a holy nation, a people belonging to God, that you may declare the praises of himwho called you out of darkness into his wonderful light I Peter 2:9 NIV

⌘

So God created man in his own image, in the image of God created he him; male and female created he them. And God blessed them and God said unto them, Be fruitful, and multiply and replenish the earth and subdue it and have dominion over the fish of the sea and over the fowl of the air, and over every living thing that moveth upon the earth. Genesis 1:27, 28

In the garden, God gave dominion and authority to both the husband and his wife. But over the years, the enemy has attempted to strip woman of the authority that God has given her. Many have been taught that God doesn't use women in ministry. Or that a woman can only be used in limited capacities. However the scripture does not support such claims.

Too often religious leaders are used by enemy to shut the mouth of God's daughter. Satan wants her muffled and stifled. Then she will not be a threat to him. He wants to tie her hands and her tongue.

However, God does use women and allow them to speak on his behalf: Miriam, the prophetess (Exodus 15:20); Deborah, the judge (Judges 4:4); Esther, the queen (the book of Esther); Anna, the prophetess (Luke 2:36); Dorcas, the servant (Acts 9:36-42); Lydia the saleswoman (Acts 16:13-15); and the daughters of Philip (Acts 21:9).

God used Priscila to co-pastor a church with her husband (I Corinthians 16:19). He also used her in concert with her husband to instruct Apollos (Acts 18:26).

God used Abigail to minister to the king to keep him from shedding blood. Abigail went against her husband's stance and followed God. She was blessed because of it. (I Samuel 25).

The ministry of the Apostle Paul also maintains the importance of women in God's kingdom purpose. In Hebrews 11, women are also listed in the hall of faith. In Romans 16, we can see that Paul commends many women, There is Phoebe, the servant of the church and helper of many (1-2); Priscilla, a fellow-worker (3-5); Mary, a hard worker (6); Junia, a relative of Paul (7); Tryphena and Tryphosa, twin sisters who were fellow-workers (12); Persis (12) and Rufus' mother whom Paul says was his (spiritual) mother, too; Julia and the sister of Nereus (15). Paul considered these ladies as legitimate ministers of the Gospel.

Further evidence points to the heart of Jesus. What was His heart toward women during his ministry on earth? Jesus had women who travelled with him and ministered to him (Luke 8:3), not just the twelve. Look at His close fellowship with Mary and Martha, the sisters of Lazarus (John 11), and Mary Magdalene (John 20); and the way in which Jesus protected women who were seen as worthless in the eyes of many men.

The attitude of Jesus toward women supports the fact that God considers us an important part of the plan for His kingdom.

And it came to pass afterward, that he went throughout every city and village preaching and shewing the glad tidings of the kingdom of God: and the twelve were with him, And *certain women*, which had been healed of evil spirits and infirmities, Mary called Magdalene, out of whom went seven devils, And Joanna the wife of Chuza Herod's steward, and Susanna, and many others, which ministered unto him of their substance St. Luke8:1-3.

When Jesus met with the Samaritan woman at the well, he revealed himself to her (St. John 4:1-42). Once she recognized him as the Messiah, she brought an entire city to Jesus. Jesus did not forbid her when she brought them to him. They came to see and believed. If she had kept quiet, the city could have possibly been lost.

Submission does not mean that a woman loses her identity as a child of God. She is a daughter of God first, before she is a wife. It doesn't matter what order the relationship started. God always assumes first position in our lives. A woman of God must retain her identity. And she is who God says that she is. Nothing more, nothing less. She can't allow the enemy to alter her image. As a born-again believer, she is granted full authority over demons and spiritual wickedness.

In fact, the scripture says she has dominion over every creeping thing. So why is she not allowed to cast them out, or preach against them, simply because she was born female?

And it shall come to pass afterward, that I will pour out my spirit upon all flesh: and your sons and your daughters shall prophesy...Joel 2:28

There are those who would fear that a woman may usurp authority over a man. To usurp authority is to take authority that is not one's own. It is not synonymous with teaching or preaching the Word. We get so twisted up and so uptight over what a woman can and cannot do. Believe it or not, men should not usurp authority, either.

We simply need to relax and let women serve their God. He is the judge of us all. Often the problem of men holding their wives back from ministry is manifested because men are unsure of themselves.

If a husband is insecure and feels jealous or threatened, it doesn't mean his wife should take a back seat. She does not have to surrender her identity because he has surrendered his. She must be confident in her relationship with the Lord. Trust God's leading. Walk in wisdom.

She does not have to prove that God uses her or that she has value. She is fully accepted in God and she just needs to rest in that fact.

There may be times when a husband tells a wife to do something and God tells her to do something different. She needs to follow the prompting of the Holy Spirit. This is not to encourage a lifestyle of rebellion against the husband.

Wives are to honor their husbands. God requires that she submit to him whether she agrees with him or not. Of course, only if it does not involve sin. However, if there is a conflict, she must follow God. Disobedience to God is sin. When God speaks to her, she must move. Just like Abigail, she could possibly save herself and the life of her family. Abigail couldn't save her husband. But she did save her household.

The highest call of any woman is a daughter of God, then wife and mother. God does not dishonor women because they are female. He does not strip them of the honor of serving him.

She has a work to do in the kingdom. She blesses Him through her service. God has instilled gifts to women. So why wouldn't He allow them to use those gifts to bring him glory?

Self-examination

1. Other than the 12 apostles, who else traveled with Jesus?

2. Before reading this chapter did you believe that God could use women?

3. Is it more honoring to God for you to use your gifts for him or not use them at all? Why/Why not?

4. What female Bible character stands out to you? Why?

5. What gifts has God given you?

Notes:

Chapter 9

Submission is....

Delight yourself also in the LORD, And He shall give you the desires of your heart. Commit your way to the LORD, Trust also in Him, And He shall bring it to pass. He shall bring forth your righteousness as the light, And your justice as the noonday. Psalm 37:4-6

⌘

This submission struggle did not begin in the 21st Century. The struggle began in the garden. Satan slithered up to the first married woman and offered her an opportunity to act independently of her God and her husband. He brought friction and conflict to the marriage; something God created as good. Sin was birthed.

Adam began accusing his wife from that time until now. Man has attempted to dominate her and treat her harshly. Eve disregarded her covering and continued to battle him for power. Both sexes were out of order. Sin brought the curse. With the curse came the struggle and marriages have been suffering ever since.

If we could just get the revelation…the curse is broken. Jesus became a curse for us. We are no longer under the curse.

Original authority is reestablished. We have full rights and claim to all benefits. Adam and his bride were created to be a team. The team can be effective on the earth, if they get God's heart on their purpose. There can be no fighting each other.

But they must turn their attention toward the one that caused this entire ruckus in the first place – Satan. He has been throwing the rock and hiding his hand.

The scriptures state, How can two walk together unless they be agreed? Amos 3:3

One will put a thousand to flight, but two, ten thousand? Deuteronomy 32:30

Together, the team is able to be far more effective than if they are divided.

There is power in agreement and unity.

The Bible teaches that, *in the Spirit,* women have equal value with men in the sight of God. This is not heresy. This is God's truth. He created the female in his image. It wasn't just the male. He gave them both dominion and charged them both to subdue and replenish the earth.

The scripture also states that, There is neither Jew nor Greek, there is neither bond nor free, there is neither male nor female: for ye are all one in Christ Jesus (Galatians 3:28).

Each of us must submit unto Jesus as our spiritual leader or head. He reigns over us all.

However, i*n the flesh,* or in a marriage, women are to be subject to their own husband's leadership. The Lord ordained that the husband would be the one that would make the final decisions in the home. He is anointed to lead his family as he submits to Christ.

In any relationship, involving two or more people, there must be a leader and final authority or their will be chaos. In the marriage, the man is the head and should guide his home and family. In the spirit, Jesus Christ is the head of His family and He guides each member as he sees fit.

Marital submission is a loving, passionate response of yielding to your spouse. It is the act of exchanging one's will for the will of a gentle God.

God has set his order for the family. He did say that the woman was subject to the man. And the man was subject to Christ. He did say that the wife ought to submit to her husband. This is a good thing.

So why do Godly women have such a hard time submitting to their husbands? One reason is that we have misunderstood what it means to submit. We've been taught a lot of falsities.

And so we rejected what we thought submission was. It seemed harsh and unfair.

The second reason is that we have not had many Godly examples. Scores of women are raised in homes without fathers. They've only known a leading matriarchal figure. So if she's never seen submission properly walked out, she only duplicates what is familiar to her.

The final reason that a woman does not submit is that she has been hurt in one way or another. So a woman will associate that hurt with being out of control. If a woman, has been raped, molested, or experienced physical or verbal abuse, in her mind, control will be her remedy. Her mind tells her that this thing can never happen again. So naturally, her response is to gain control to avoid the hurt.

How does a woman learn submission? Of course, she first needs to gain an understanding. She should prayerfully seek and study the heart of God on this subject.

Secondly, healing is often the next step on the journey to submission. She must change the way she views men. She must engage the Lord in the process of healing her wounded heart. And become vulnerable again.

The third step is moving in obedience. The scripture says that wives should obey their husbands (Titus 2:5). Obedience and submission are not the same word. Obedience is an act of compliance. Submission is a heart of compliance.

We start out with steps of obedience and prayerfully end in loving submission.

Submission is emancipation. In the family relationship, God puts all heavy burdens on the shoulders of men. And a wife simply has to come alongside him in support as his helper. She doesn't have the tough job of leading the family. It is her husband's responsibility. When she totally understands this, she will realize how liberating submission is. God asks for her submission to bless her. He didn't intend for submission to be an evil word.

Submission is the willingness to trust in a loving God. Take Him at His word. He is for us and not against us. So if he tells us to submit, it is to our advantage. It is a blessing not a curse.

Submission brings order in the family. It produces humility and harmony in familial relationships.

It is our most honorable privilege to submit our lives to the King of all kings. He is so amazingly good to us, that we are provoked to pour out our love on Him. His love is immeasurable toward us and we know we cannot match it. But if we even aim to come close, then we must demonstrate our love through our yieldedness.

So when He says submit yourselves to your husband as unto the Lord, it should be done in reverence to the One who asks. We are to submit to our husbands even when we do not agree or understand. We must submit when we don't like what is being requested (as long as it doesn't violate the things we discussed in the previous chapters.) Read I Peter 3:1, Ephesians 5:22 and Colossians 3:18.

Our husbands will give account of their leadership. And we

will give account of how well we followed. We need to remember that our submission is aimed directly at our Gentle Redeemer.

As we go forward, let us fully comprehend what submission is and what it isn't. I hope you won't stop here in your quest to understand what submission is and what it isn't. I hope you will pray and seek the Lord for revelation on submission. Search the scriptures fervently to get his heart beat on this subject. Because when we have God's heart on the matter, we will say...submission is a beautiful word.

Self-examination

1. Why does God ask us to submit?

2. In what cases are you not to submit?

3. What is true submission?

4. Explain Ephesians 5:21-22.

5. What have you learned since you started reading this book?

Notes:

⌘

A Prayer of Submission

My Dearest Lord,

Thank you for creating me in your image and likeness. I embrace and celebrate my femininity. Thank you for the gifts, talents, and abilities that you have invested in me. May I always give them back to you in loving appreciation. Help me, Father, to never let my femininity be used as an excuse or hindrance from serving you.

Lord, help me to be all that you intended for me to be. Give me wisdom and grace that far exceed my years. Help me to walk in courage to make right choices. And teach me how to be bold in my service to you.

Create in me a heart of humility. So that I will walk in holy submission to you at all times, giving honor and reverence to my husband, as unto you. May I never overstep my boundaries. And may I never withdraw my service to you. Help me to rightly discern how to govern myself at all times.

May my heart be wholly submitted to you in everything I do, say and think. In Jesus' name, I pray. Amen.

Suggested Scripture Readings:

Genesis 3:15

And I will put enmity between you and the woman, and between your offspring and hers; he will crush your head, andyou will strike his heel."

Joel 2: 28-29

"And afterward, I will pour out my Spirit on all people. Your sons and daughters will prophesy, your old men will dream dreams, your young men will see visions. Even on my servants, both men and women, I will pour out my Spirit in those days.

Galatians 3:28

There is neither Jew nor Greek, slave nor free, male nor female, for you are all one in Christ Jesus.

Judges 4:4 NIV

Deborah, a prophetess, the wife of Lappidoth, was leading Israel at that time.

Ephesians 5:21-25,28

"Wives, submit to your own husbands, as to the Lord. For the husband is head of the wife, as also Christ is head of the church; and He is the Savior of the body. Therefore, just as the church is subject to Christ, so let the wives be to their own husbands in everything. Husbands, love your wives, just as Christ also loved the church and gave Himself for her"

Ephesians 5:33

"Nevertheless let each one of you in particular so love his own wife as himself, and let the wife *see* that she respects *her* husband."

Colossians 3:18

Wives, submit yourselves unto your own husbands, as it is fit in the Lord.

1 Peter 3:1-4

"Wives, likewise, be submissive to your own husbands, that even if some do not obey the word, they, without a word, may be won by the conduct of their wives, when they observe your chaste conduct accompanied by fear. Do not let your adornment be merely outward—arranging the hair, wearing gold, or putting on fine apparel—rather let it be the hidden person of the heart, with the incorruptible beauty of a gentle and quiet spirit, which is very precious in the sight of God."

1 Peter 5:5, 6

"Likewise you younger people, submit yourselves to your elders. Yes, all of you be submissive to one another, and be clothed with humility, for 'God resists the proud, But gives grace to the humble.' "

Romans 16:1

"I commend to you our sister *Phoebe*, who is a servant of the church which is at Cenchrea; that you receive her in the Lord in a manner worthy of the saints, and that you help her in whatever matter she may have need of you; for she herself has also been a helper of many, and of myself as well (Rom. 16:1-2; emphasis added).

About the Author

Crystal Jones is the love and hearthrob of Apostle Oscar Jones. The couple joyfully celebrates 40 years of marriage. Crystal is the loving mother of 5 adult children and 3 bonus children(in-laws) and the beaming grandmother of 11.

She is a speaker, minister, mentor and author. She has ministered all over the country. She has been the featured guest on many radio programs and a television program, She has authored more than 20 books.

She is the founder of the Fearless Women's Conferences. She ministers to women all over the country.

Crystal is Co-Publisher of Destiny House Publishing, LLC. Along with her husband, she is co founder of **Marriage For A Lifetime Ministries** and she and her husband are apostolic overseers to **Agape International Association of Churches and Para-churches**. They have a unique Aquila & Priscilla anointing where they minister together as one voice.

Crystal is wildly in love with her Lord and Savior, Jesus Christ. She is fully committed to her relationship with Him and counts it an amazing privilege and an honor. She aspires to help others experience the same type of intimacy with her Kind King.

To contact the author:

Marriage For A Lifetime Ministries

P.O. Box 19774 Detroit, MI 48219

404.993.0830

www.marriage4alifetime.org

Email: jones@marriage4alifetime.org

www.ingramcontent.com/pod-product-compliance
Lightning Source LLC
LaVergne TN
LVHW051704080426
835511LV00017B/2728